A Fountain of Dreams

Haiku - Tanka - Senryu - Shisan Renku

Dr. Kathleen P. Decker, Editor

Dedicated to all the poets and photographers
who made this book possible:

Susan Bennett

Jan Bohall

Susan Bornstein

Christine Brooks

Terry Cox-Joseph

Jacqueline Davey

Kathleen P. Decker

Lucy Tu Freeman

Mark Fryburg

Gwen Hickling

iStock

Mirtha Toyo King

Joan Lunsford

Chitra Mohla

Susan Rexroad

Edward Sadtler

Margie Wildblood

Carolyn F. Wyatt

Table of Contents   Page(s)

Table of Contents

Table of Contents   **Page(s)**

Table of Contents

Page(s)

Shisan Renku Section (continued)

Editor's Note

This book is a compilation of American-style Japanese poetry written by George Mason students in the Osher Lifelong Learning Institute Program Summer, 2025.

We first took on a "finish-the-haiku" challenge to break the ice. I wrote the first two lines, and invited participants to write a third line to link to the first two, and shift the scene and complete a haiku. We did another fun exercise later in the course where we took our original "finish-the-haiku" snowy mountain haiku and added two longer lines to make them into tanka, to introduce the concept of tanka, with fun results!

Subsequent sections of this book were created as participants gained familiarity with haiku and tanka writing forms. They launched their own forays, exploring nature with haiku, and wrote senryu on the subject of global warming. Then they added human connections through tanka.

The final phase of the course centered on crafting collaborative Shisan Renku (12-link) renku in groups of 3-4 poets, using traditional Japanese guidelines. These include: use of all four seasons in the poem, using each season only once, including a moon verse, a blossom verse, and two love verses. The love links must represent two different types of love. As with all renku poems, each verse must link to the previous, yet shift to another topic. The poem must not be a narrative, nor tell a coherent story, which was initially a challenge for Western poets. Ultimately, their Shisan renku creations are a wonderful set of poems that crowned our weeks together! It turns out we had many gifted photographers to illustrate our poems, as well. Please enjoy this creative endeavor as much as we did creating it!

~Dr. Kathleen P. Decker, Editor, Instructor

雪の山俳句

Snowy Mountain Haiku

"Mt. Fuji" Photo by Jacqueline Davey

snowy mountain
along the tree line
elusive leopard glides
             Chitra Mohla

snowy mountain
along the tree line
nature changes mind
                Edward Sadtler

snowy mountain
along the treeline
a bear pees
             Joan Lunsford

snowy mountain
shrouded trees shudder
powdery mist
               Susan Rexroad

snowy mountain
along the treeline
white treetop spires
            Margie Wildblood

"Mt. Fuji"
Photo by Jacqueline Davey

snowy mountain
along the treeline
water reflects shadows
        Lucy Tu Freeman

                snowy mountain
                along the treeline
                hungry lion lurks
                        Carolyn F. Wyatt

snowy mountains
along the treeline glides
a white owl
        Jan Bohall

                snowy mountain
                along the treeline
                split by an avalanche
                        Gwen Hickling

snowy mountain
along the treeline
foxes sniff for rodents
        Margie Wildblood

"Cross-Country,"
Photo by Jacqueline Davey

mountain snow cap
above the tree line
frozen moon reflected
      Susan Bennett

      snowy mountain
      along the tree line
      shadows of eagle wings
            Jacqueline Davey

snowy mountain
along the treeline
mountain goats mate
      Mark Fryburg

      snowy mountain
      along the treeline
      bear prints in white
            Margie Wildblood

snowy mountain
along the treeline
ravens soar and dive
      Susan Bornstein

"Winter Creek, Utah,"
Photo by Jacqueline Davey

雪山短歌

Snowy Mountain Tanka

"Jasper National Park" by Lucy Tu Freeman

snowy mountain
its dark treeline
split by an avalanche
      trees strewn at crazy angles
      like I just bowled a strike
            Gwen Hickling

      snowy mountain
      along the treeline
      a bear pees
            I search for a white path
            and the culprit
                  Joan Lunsford

snowy mountain
along the tree line
nature changes mind
      so do two shooters
      longing for fire
            Edward Sadtler

      snowy mountain
      along the treeline
      ravens soar and dive
            each morning I ask myself—
            have we learned from what we see?
                  Susan Bornstein

"Lake Louise" Photo by Lucy Tu Freeman

snowy mountain
along the tree line glides
a white owl
      startles late day trekker
      binoculars at the ready
            Jan Bohall

snowy mountain
along the treeline
water reflects shadows
      I'm in awe and thankful
      …still able to hike
            Lucy Tu Freeman

snowy mountain
along the tree line
shadows of eagle wings
      bungie jumping
      tourists scream with joy
            Jacqueline Davey

snowy mountain
shrouded trees shudder
powdery mist
      my faith in
      America shaken
           Susan Rexroad

snowy mountain
      along the tree line
      elusive leopard glides
            ghost of mountain in decline
            man's hubris-his nemesis
                Chitra Mohla

"Cadomin Lake" Photo
by Lucy Tu Freeman

俳句／川柳

Haiku/Senryu

"Bear in Jasper National Park" Photo by Lucy Tu Freeman

Winter

ponder the snow
on Kilimanjaro
understand purity
      Edward Sadtler

      glacier mountain tops
      bring flowing valley river
      sunshine becomes rainstorm
            Lucy Tu Freeman

blizzard blows
wet snow clumps fur
wolves' coats heavy
      Margie Wildblood

      late snowfall
      catches in crevices stays
      into July
            Jan Bohall

"Mt. Vimy, Waterton Lakes, Canada,"
Photo by Margie Wildblood

Spring

spring snow bends branches
my lover's stare
melted by noon
      Mark Fryburg

      dew falls
      lovers awaken
      drenched
            Edward Sadtler

wide-mouth bowl
sun shower burst
birdbath open
      Susan Rexroad

      a fountain of dreams
      sleeping under the stars
      in a village by the river
            Chitra Mohla

magnolia blooms
lush fragrance fills warm air
bird drama unfolds
      Susan Bornstein

      rainstorms awaken
      green sprouts
      outdoors we go
            Margie Wildblood

"Blooming Rose"
Photo by Margie Wildblood"

spring moon
rests on granite hills
out of reach
`   Mark Fryburg

          morels' earthy scent—
          messages spring's arrival.
          risotto calls
                    Susan Bornstein

waterfall
whispering today
roared yesterday
          Edward Sadtler

Summer

heat wave
garden invasion
Japanese beetles
      Mark Fryburg

      dead flesh
      vultures feast
      unfathomable heat
             Joan Lunsford

orange day lilies
only one blossom remains
the doe eats that, too
      Gwen Hickling

      blackberries
      sweet, fat
      bears gorge
             Carolyn F. Wyatt

sun flares horizon
at dusk and dawn
why do cows come home?
      Edward Sadtler

"Mule Deer"
Photo by Margie Wildblood

wild hair uncontained
in relentless summer air
I resemble Bigfoot
　　　　Susan Bornstein

Summer

June gutter-flooders
one upon another
soon, fish in the streets
      Edward Sadtler

      heat bakes dry earth
      moist breeze tickles limp blooms
      thumping rain delayed
            Susan Bennett

      deep beneath the waves
      pufferfish sculpts sand circles
      to woo his mate
            Susan Bornstein

"Tire Swing"
Photo by Margie Wildblood

Fall

twilight descends
into purple-blue sky
fireflies spin stars of gold
       Chitra Mohla

       red maples drape over ferns
       paths cross moss bridges
       tea house awaits full moon
          Jacqueline Davey

clear lake
V-shaped geese fly
to the rose garden
       Mirtha Toyo King

       tide pool
       dark shadows appear
       sea turtles graze
          Mark Fryburg

trees bow
to the Gods who make of them
home
       Edward Sadtler

autumn light lingers   I
pawpaws hang from leafy limbs
sweetness slowly falls
        Susan Bornstein

"Tree Trail"
Photo by Margie Wildblood

短歌

TANKA

"Stargazer Lilly" Photo by Margie Wildblood

orange day lilies
only one blossom remains
the doe eats that, too
        for the first time I see
        a use for firearms
                        Gwen Hickling

fireflies' light
ephemeral days of warmth
snow by the window
        years gone by without a trace
        mingled pang of wistfulness
                        Chitra Mohla

cool azure pool
midday sun blazes
goldfish gasps for air
        burnt by sun
        I take refuge in water
                        Edward Sadtler

"Brigham Young House, Utah"
Photo by Margie Wildblood

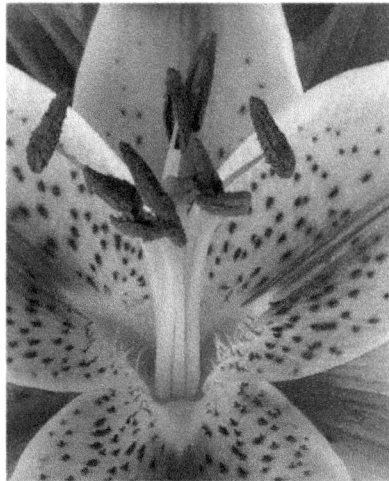

"Stargazer Lilly" Photo
by Margie Wildblood

red maples drape ferns
shed leaves onto moss bridges
over smooth water
        she unveils the gift
        tea house ceremony
                    Jacqueline Davey

        scrawny peach tree
        offers ripe and rotting fruit
        to all comers
                skinny teenagers
                sport skinnier thongs
                        Carolyn F. Wyatt

"Miyajima Island,"
Photo by Jacqueline Davey

mountain glacier
sends a river to the valley
sunshine becomes rainstorm
    my old bones crave
    hot mint tea and a warm bath
          Lucy Tu Freeman

    large, leafy trees in our yard
    branchier each year
    grow a foot a season
        where have the years gone-
        my hair thinner each year
            Joan Lunsford

warm honey drips
from laden combs—bees labor
quietly for all
    so much waste in the world
    so many idle humans
         Susan Bornstein

"Great Falls of the Potomac
#3" Photo by Margie Wildblood

bright radiance of cardinals
ruby bodies warmed by sun
their song awakens the day
       I stir in cool sheets
         Where are you now?
            Susan Bornstein

at family beach house
the one-legged seagull
begs at window
         I ask my mother
         for more oatmeal
             Mark Fryburg

grey mourning doves
shake heads joined at the beak
prelude to mating
        bouncy bobbleheads
        remind me of you
             Susan Bennett

"Burke Lake Geese" Photo by Lucy Tu Freeman

ocean twirls
blue white tendrils
imbue sunbaked shells
      upward spirals in my
      inner cosmos
            Susan Rexroad

      night sky blackens
      sudden thunder
      atmosphere inverts
            my nation's government
            falls into chaos
                 Mark Fryburg

male firefly swoops
flashes invitation to mate
females blink consent
      less bashful
      a girl kisses her boy
            Jan Bohall

Photo credit: iStock image

perfumed orange tree
bending low with hidden pests
leaves crust and drift down
    always sweeping green carpet—
    you fight and so will I
                     Susan Bornstein

invisible breezes
show themselves making
summer leaves flutter
    I want to shimmy
    along with the leaves
                 Gwen Hickling

"Queen Butterfly" Photo by Margie Wildblood

川柳: 地球温暖化

Senryu: Global Warming

"Wizard Island, Crater Lake" Photo by Mark Fryburg

June gutter-flooders
one upon another
woe to lawn cutters
                    Edward Sadtler

veiled mothers
cradle starving infants
no milk, less comfort
                    Carolyn F. Wyatt

forest raped for lumber
no cool shade from sun
black asphalt steams
                    Margie Wildblood

hot howling winds
hurl flaming sticks and twigs
homeowner's plight
                    Chitra Mohla

"Jasper National Park Wildfire 2024"
Photo by Lucy Tu Freeman

bike-path bustles
February eighty degrees
trampled green shoots
        Susan Rexroad

ongoing warming
from green toward orange red
felt by living things
        Lucy Tu Freeman

coral color fades
clownfish search where home once was
humans gasp for air
        Susan Bornstein

America boils
we evacuate
invade Canada
        Mark Fryburg

        baked Alaska
        served up
        to climate-deniers
                Edward Sadtler

Iceland tourists
overrun by mosquitoes
malaria follows
        Mark Fryburg

        unendurable heat
        could stop us cold
        global warning
                Gwen Hickling

"Yellowstone Lake Hotel Porch,"
Photo by Margie Wildblood

"Wizard Island, Crater Lake"
Photo by Mark Fryburg

seawaters warm
more severe storms yet
we drive on
       Jan Bohall

      dear children
      oceans we leave to you
      floating plastic
            Jacqueline Davey

bright yellow sun
ocean waves brought opera
into my dreams
      Mirtha Toyo King

      clogging ocean highways
      no sign of disintegration
      plastic debris
            Joan Lunsford

"Children on Beach", Photo by Margie Wildblood

連

句

SHISAN RENKU

"Bleeding Heart" Photo by Margie Wildblood

"Blitz"
By Mark Fryburg, Susan Bennett, and
Lucy Tu Freeman

beetles blitz garden
July thunderstorm answers
attackers washed away
    MF

    gardener breathes a sigh of relief
    when the mortgage is paid
        SB

autumn wind
maple and oak leaves
fallen, falling
    LTF

    the air chills
    we look to the October moon
        MF

a dog walks
on falling snow
in a foxes' tracks
    LTF

    children chase the dog
    schools are closed
        MF

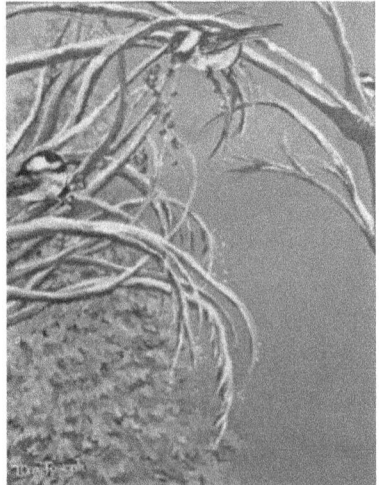

"Winter Chickadee" Photo by Terry Cox-Joseph

first green leaves
serviceberry blossoms
hay fever attack
          MF

          love in flowers, embracing
          the innocent and pure
                    LTF

blue lake
cool gentle breeze, on the face
of a quacking duck
                    LTF

          fly dances on lake
          fisherman gets trout!
                    MF

lifetime dance partners
forms change
love sees beyond
                    LTF

          composing session over
          excitement remains
                    LTF

"Silver Threads"
By Chitra Mohla, Jacqueline Davey, Joan Lunsford, and Margie Wildblood

dotted silver threads
dropped from heaven
adorn fields and valley
CM

      strands woven among us
      connect over kitchen table
      JD

trees grow taller
oaks' acorns abound with food
squirrels can't wait
JL

      golden moon, shining bright
      across land and sea, magical sight
      CM

glow of snow scene
landscapes of frigid ice
nights of flannel warmth
JD

      silent whispers through the pines
      time for quiet reflection
      JL

white water lilies
profusion of confetti
awaken at dawn
      CM

      wedding bouquet
      floats before white dreams
      JD

abundance of life
hummingbirds hover
bees-nature's gardeners
      CM

      fairies visit the vineyard
      vaulting in colorful capes
      CM

comfort years
age to reminisce
beautiful youth
      CM

      light fades
      turn to home
      MW

"Lake Louise, Canada"
Photo by Margie Wildblood

"Golden"
By Susan Rexroad, Carolyn F. Wyatt, Kathleen P. Decker, and Edward Sadtler

sunflowers seek
nourishment of day's beams
petals' gold deepens
SR

California miner descends
to seek his fortune
CW

rainy redwood forest
leaves underfoot turning
the sound of an eagle
KPD

harvest moon, couple strolls
wrapped in amber
SR

snowy owl glides
swiftly silently swoops
misses mouse
CW

you left little behind
we mourn together
KPD

tight buds open
chipmunk awakens
fox sniffs prey and blooms
SR

we pass in the street
your perfume entices
CW

trees rise from shade
shelter undergrowth
a cat pounces
ES

she leapt when splashed
by the incoming wave
SR

feline, canine
sit in sunny patch
touch noses
CW

streets full of people
going their merry way
ES

Photo: Image credit iStock

Almost Ready

By Margie Wildblood, Chitra Mohla, and Jacqueline Davey

fawn follows doe
almost ready
to leave fold
       MW

      wander sun-dappled forests
      hikers seek a picnic site
      JD

vines of golden grapes
mashed in oak barrels
vintner's delight
       CM

      full moon's silvery rays
      fields of frosted pumpkins
      JD

ice framed windows
glowing evening embers
rocking chair naps
       CM

      dreams of white shiny hills
      snowball fights in crunchy meadows
      JD

"Deer" Photo by Christine Brooks

angelic dogwoods
thrive in warm sunshine
herald new life
              MW

        innocent April tenderness
        deep flames of affection
              MW

abandoned orchard
exudes aroma
of decaying apples
              CM

        far across the field
        old farmer wanders aimlessly
              JD

love lasts
if nourished to mature
interest wanes
              MW

        at the crossroads
        until we meet again
              JD

CONTRIBUTORS BIOS AND INDEX

CONTRIBUTORS BIOS:

Susan Bennett (she/her) is a poet, activist and ritualist, leading women's spirit circles in Northern Virginia for two decades. Her poems have been published in *Ekphrastic Review, Amethyst Review, Gargoyle Magazine, Rise Up Review,Artemis Journal, Nap Lit, Eternal Haunted Summer, Mslexia* and the *Menopause Anthology,* published by Arachne Press.

Jan Bohall moderated the Poetry Workshop at the Osher Lifelong Learning Institute at George Mason University for many years. Retired from public health nursing, she has produced a chapbook of her poems, *Tasting Life Twice.* Her work has been published in various periodicals, and she has won awards from the Poetry Society of Virginia.

Susan Bornstein spent 30 years in international development nonprofits promoting economic opportunity. Since retiring, she supports local social sector organizations and explores creative forms, including a first effort to write Japanese-style poetry. She enjoyed the experiment and now finds joy in a daily haiku practice, shared with her husband in Northern Virginia.

Christine Brooks was a programmer for 30 years and then a technical writer for 12 years. In retirement, she enjoys walking and taking pictures along the way.

Terry Cox-Joseph is Past President of the Poetry Society of Virginia and is a former newspaper reporter and editor. From 1994-2004 she was the coordinator for the annual Christopher Newport University Writers' Conference and Contest. An award-winning poet, she has been published in *Northern Virginia Review, Allegro and Chiron Review* among others. She displays and sells her watercolors, acrylics and oils at On The Hill Gallery in Yorktown.

Jacqueline Davey lives in Oakton, Virginia. Following a career in book publishing and marketing, she now enjoys volunteer activities and travel, outdoor sports and classical piano. She joined the OLLI community in 2022,

CONTRIBUTORS BIOS, CONT'D.:

Jacqueline Davey, cont'd.:

and now also studies with George Mason University's Creative Writing Program. She has been published in several journals; she was also a winner in the Fairfax County Library's 2023 Poetry Contest and the 2025 Poetry Society of Virginia awards.

Dr. Kathleen P. Decker is a prize-winning poet and is President of the Poetry Society of Virginia. She has been a member of the Haiku Society of America since 1996. She has authored three books of Japanese haiku and tanka, and edited two haiku anthologies, *My Neighbor's Life* and *On Crimson Wings.* She has also written several books of Western poetry and edited four Western poetry anthologies.

Lucy Tu Freeman is a retired Family and Consumer Science educator from Fairfax County Public Schools. She holds a Master of Science in Nutrition from The University of the Incarnate Word. A lifelong learner and novice poet, she finds Japanese nature poetry's simplicity and brevity both challenging and gratifying. Born in China, she is writing a memoir about her journey to the US at 15, leaving Cambodia behind.

Mark Fryburg has been a journalist, PR man and flight instructor. Retirement revealed his passion for poetry. Last year, several state and national competitions honored his work. Mark says maybe it's his short attention span, or the challenge of packing a great deal into a small space, but haiku is his new love! Mark lives near Roanoke, Virginia, with his bride Laura.

Gwen Hickling is a happily retired software developer who has always loved language and learning. She enjoys looking into things that are not everyday knowledge, like the differences between the haiku and senryu forms. Nature inspires her with joy, humor and awe. A Northern Virginia native, she lives in Vienna with a very nice guy.

CONTRIBUTORS' BIOS, CONT'D.:

Mirtha Toyo King is a Japanese American born in Peru, a retired Spanish teacher with a deep love for poetry. Inspired by her mother and their shared heritage, she is exploring Japanese poetry as a way to reconnect with her roots and express herself through language and tradition.

Joan Lunsford, a native of the Washington DC area, taught string orchestra in Fairfax County Public Schools for 30 years. She presently plays violin in the Manassas Symphony Orchestra, and enjoys playing piano as well. Joan loves writing poems and prose via OLLI workshops, and even got published several times. She and her husband, Rich, love traveling. Australia is next.

Chitra Mohla is a retired microbiologist and health information technology consultant. In retirement she has found joy in writing poetry. Japanese-style poetry opens up a world of imagination and creativity, a form of happy therapy.

Susan Rexroad began writing poetry at stop lights, scrawling down words needing to come to the page. These poetic visitations prompted her to study the craft. She moderates and teaches poetry for the Osher Lifetime Learning Institute. In 2025, she won Fairfax County's Poetic Musing's contest for free verse.

Edward Sadtler is a retired furniture salesman, who, to keep his sanity, has been writing poetry since his teens. Along life's way, he was fortunate enough to "marry up," and, with his wife, enjoys two now adult children and two grandchildren, all of whom are smarter than he is. Gratitude plays a big role in his life.

Margie Wildblood grew up in a log cabin in southwest Virginia. She earned degrees in English, Psychology and Counseling. Since retiring from Northern Virginia Community College as a counselor and faculty member, she participates in and moderates writing workshops with the Osher Lifelong Learning Institute at George Mason University.

CONTRIBUTORS' BIOS, CONT'D.:

Carolyn F. Wyatt is a retired Intelligence Community information officer who traveled widely in that position. She has an MA in Spanish from Indiana University and aspires to be a poet and a wise woman.

INDEX

Contributors   Page(s)

www.ingramcontent.com/pod-product-compliance
Lightning Source LLC
Chambersburg PA
CBHW032053040426
42449CB00007B/1093